Journey

Finding the Hidden Gems

Limaonen Imchen

© Limaonen Imchen 2016

Published by
Limaonen Imchen

First edition 2016

ISBN: 9789352584406

Illustrations by Longmo Jamir
longmojamir@gmail.com

Cover design by Rizen Longchar
riz_lcr@post.com

Powered by
Pothi.com
http://pothi.com

All Scripture quotations are taken from the Holy Bible.

Dedicated to

all those

who have been a part of my journey

There is a purpose

Limaonen Imchen in the book, *Journey: Finding the Hidden Gems*, invites the readers to take a look at his "Journey" by sharing a couple of instances that contributed the most towards his transformation from a frustrated and angry teenager to a patient and God fearing man.

Throughout the book, he reiterates his purpose for sharing his life story which is to guide the young people in search for a direction and thereby, help them understand the purpose of life. Young people often misunderstand, but at the same time, they are also the most misunderstood; so this book comes along at an opportune time, as today, the majority of Nagaland's population comprise of the youth. This young population more than ever needs leaders who can motivate and help them discover their true worth, mobilize and channelize their gifts towards the construction of a loving, peaceful and God fearing society.

The book powerfully drives home the fact that life is not easy. The title of the book clearly states that these "gems" about life is hidden and one has to search for it. The process of being disciplined by our heavenly Father for His divine purpose is arduous, slow and beyond our comprehension.

By highlighting some of his own experiences, he urges the readers to be patient, to keep a willing heart and an open mind, and to be hopeful in the Lord so that one will not miss the illumination that will be bestowed upon an individual at the end of it all.

Limayangla Pongener,
Assistant Professor,
Sao Chang Govt. College,
Tuensang

God does perform miracles!

Some of these miracles are spectacular, like saving our lives or sending us into the world. Some are more subtle, like changing our character and transforming our inner person.

God's means are unusual and often unexpected: changes in location, a leaking roof, unpleasant tasks and questioned identity. Who am I when the things that have defined me are stripped away?

Only time and reflection allow us to understand God's purposes in our lives.

Limaonen Imchen invites us to enter into reflection with him by telling us his story – in a number of individual stories. Each one of these exemplifies an area of life that we tend to take for granted – until we are challenged to let it go and surrender it to our God and Maker.

In HIS hands they are molded into something new and beautiful, to glorify HIS name.

I encourage you to follow Lima's journey – and to respond to his inspiration to embark on your own.

**Katharina Richardson,
Kaiserslautern, Germany**

Contents

Foreword   (11)

Journey   (13)

Indian but not Indians   (15)

Is War an Answer for Peace?   (21)

My Mother Suffered for Me   (24)

Do You Have a Dream
for a Better Tomorrow?   (28)

Moving Four Times in Two Years   (32)

Lessons Learnt from a Tree   (49)

I Played a Lullaby for my Friend   (52)

Drowning my Attitude   (57)

My Journey towards Germany   (61)

An Encounter with a Boy
from the Amazon Rainforest   (68)

Journey Well   (73)

Foreword

Experience is a great teacher. When we reflect on our lives and our experiences, both positive and negative, we can often learn valuable lessons. Those who learn from their experiences are often able to avoid future mistakes in life, and can reap the abundant life we are promised in Jesus Christ. But there is a problem. Life is simply too short to learn every lesson we need to learn on the basis of our own experiences. That is why the wisest people come to understand the value of learning from the experiences of others. In the Bible in I Corinthians 10:11 the Apostle Paul writes: *"Now these things happened to them as an example, and they were written for our instruction…"* Paul understands that God not only gives us experiences, but also gives us the experiences of others through which we can learn.

My dear friend Limaonen Imchen, though young, has already lived an incredible life filled with many experiences. He grew up in Nagaland, a place filled with amazing history and abundant wonder. He has since travelled everywhere from the tropical rainforests of Amazonia to the vibrant cities of Europe. He has undergone a multitude of different adventures and also shared many of life's ordinary simple moments. But more importantly Lima has reflected on those experiences, learned valuable lessons from them, and now has written many of them so that others can learn from them too. These writings are a wonderful gift to those wise men and women who understand the value of learning through the experiences of others. I learn much from Lima every time we have a chance to be together, and I know you too will gain much insight into life as you enjoy these stories and the wisdom they impart.

Life is a wonderful gift. I hope you are living it to the fullest. I also hope that you enjoy sharing in these stories from Lima's life, stories that are designed to give life as well. The Apostle Paul also said in Romans 15:4 – "*For everything that was written in the past was written to teach us, so that through the endurance taught in the Scriptures and the encouragement they provide we might have hope.*" My prayer is that you might find hope in these words!

Many Blessings,
Dr. Max A. Wilkins
President/CEO – The Mission Society.
Norcross, Georgia, USA

Journey

As I set about writing this book, my original thought was to write a book similar to my first: Nobody to Somebody. I thought about incorporating more testimonies of people who have done amazing things, as well as a few stories of my own experiences, but as I started writing I found the direction of my book was changing.

My aim as an author and an orator is to reach out to people, especially young people, encouraging and motivating them in whatever way I can. I know life as a teenager can be tough. There's a lot of pressure from family, school and society, and there are a lot of changes occurring in the body at the same time. Emotions are all up and down and many teens struggle with self-esteem, self-worth and identity issues. My goal is to help them to have hope and believe in themselves.

So, my book took a different turn as I was writing, and I decided to base this book entirely upon my own experiences. Each chapter highlights a different time in my life when I faced something new or difficult, and each chapter tells a bit about what I learnt through each episode.

I hope that by sharing these moments– the hard times, the good times, the exciting or scary times, and the lessons that I learnt– some of my readers may be challenged, changed and motivated through the stories.

Indian but not Indians

(Dedicated to every Naga who had faced or is facing the same situation as me)

"You're Indian?"

"Yes I am."

"No, you don't look like an Indian."

"Well, I am an Indian."

This kind of conversation is one of the most common conversations I come across every time I go out of my state, Nagaland. Be it South India, North India, or Central India, or even in other countries, this is the most common question or conversation I have when I meet people for the first time.

When I was at school we went to Goa for an excursion. Travelling out of Nagaland for the first time, and going to Goa of all places, meant my excitement and expectations were high. I imagined having the opportunity to talk to some white people and obviously having some photos taken with the tourists near the beach, and I couldn't wait to see the sea for the first time, having spent my entire life surrounded by mountains. As we disembarked from the train in Goa, in the second week of January 2000, we were surrounded by a bunch of children begging us for money. We gave them a few rupees and expected them to be satisfied with that and walk away, but instead they started asking us for our own currency, not Indian currency. So, we tried to explain to them that we were from Nagaland in North East India, to which they replied, "Oh, China." It took a while to explain that we really were from India.

Since that day I've heard the same question repeatedly "You are Indian?" whenever I tell someone I'm from India.

I take this identity issue as a blessing as well a curse. I'm proud that the looks of my people are unique and gives us our own identity, but at the same time, it can sometimes make me feel like a foreigner in my own land. It can be particularly frustrating and irritating when someone calls me Chinese or a Chinky in my own country, or even Tibetan sometimes.

Questions about being Indian became very common when I went to Germany. I was going to study there and people at my school were expecting an Indian to join them. When I arrived, many of the other students (who are now my friends) found it hard to believe that I was the person from India. In one incident, one of my friends asked me "I know you are from India but genetically from which country do you belong?" It was hilarious. In another incident we were having dinner with a group of visiting students when one of the girls asked one of my friends "I heard there is an Indian in the school, but I can't find him, where is he?"

My friend pointed at me and said "That's him."

The lady replied "Oh, nice" before continuing to eat her food. Later, on a more serious note, she asked the same question again, so again my friend pointed at me and told her that it's me. When she received the same answer she stared at me for a little while in amazement, before directing the next questions at me. "Are you serious?" and "Is your mum from another Asian country or did your family migrate to India or something?"

The worst experience I had was when I visited Brazil. As I stepped out of the airport I saw a lot of people that looked like my own people and thought that maybe they were tourists like me. It took me a while to realise they were actually Brazilian and I had a hard time trying to explain to them that I wasn't Brazilian, I was Indian, and then why I looked so different to the "normal" Indian person that people usually imagined. Carrying an Indian passport but looking more Asian was another challenging but funny experience every time I went through Immigration as I visited each country.

As a result of my identity issue as Indian (both in India as well as abroad) I came up with a good way of explaining where I am from. "I come from a place where the people look Asian; they dress like Europeans; they sing like Nightingales; most people mistake us for being Chinese; the place looks like the Amazon rainforest; if you drive on the highway it feels like you're having an off-road experience; by country we're Indian; by religion we're Head Hunters converted to Christianity and all that combined describes my place known as Nagaland. That's why I say we're "Indian but not Indians."

A brief history of Nagaland turning from Head Hunting to Christianity

Nagaland is a mixture of various tribes with different languages. According to history, our people (The Nagas) only encountered the outside world when the British Empire tried to conquer Angami (one of the Naga tribes) territory, which is presently the district known as Kohima, the capital of our state, Nagaland. The second contact the Nagas had with foreigners was when the Gospel of Christ reached the Naga Hills from Ahom land, through Ao (one of the Naga tribes) territory, in the mid-19th century. Since then Christianity has made tremendous advances in Nagaland. According to history Reverend Miles Bronson was the first Missionary who came to Nagaland. However, Christianity spread in Nagaland only after the coming of Reverend E. W. Clark, a Missionary from America.

According to the stories I've heard from our elders and learnt at school, when Dr. E. W. Clark came to Nagaland, our people were still Head Hunters. They were fighting between villages and showing their strength as warriors by the number of heads they could get. But the missionaries were determined to spread the Gospel. They lived with the tribal people, ate and worked with them and slowly they led our people to accept Jesus as our Saviour, which ended Head Hunting practices.

Is War an Answer for Peace?

I grew up in a place that was gripped with fear. Often our family could hear people being threatened, tortured or even killed. There was always tension in my small town of Mokokchung under the state of Nagaland, India, during the early 1990s. Sometimes we heard the sound of gunfire while we were in class, and at other times we'd have to run away from our homes in search of a safer place to hide. We never knew when a group of militants might come and check our houses. Sometimes we'd have to get up in the middle of the night and stand in a corner while the army searched every inch of our home for arms or any documents that might be belong to different militant groups.

The worst thing was being stuck somewhere, unable to get home for hours and hours, just because there was a fight happening between different militant groups somewhere in our neighbourhood. Everywhere we went we'd hear the sound of gunshots and the news of people being killed.

Life was full of fear and many times we lived at the mercy of the militants, not knowing what might happen if they became suspicious of us for any reason.

So, growing up I always wished that one day I would get to experience a peaceful life with no fear of war, extortion, kidnappings and the like. But things worsened as I began to realise that the whole world was full of hatred, conflict, envy, greed, ruthlessness and selfishness, and peopled by power mongers. Whenever I looked at the news it was full of reports of fighting, murders, attacks and so on. And the really sad part is that it's still happening: our world is getting worse and worse.

What is wrong with our world? Will we ever find peace? Is war the only solution? Why do so many people have to die? Is it effective to declare war in order to bring about lasting peace? Will it really bring concord to our land?

Does not love drive out all fear? Is not love the answer, bringing as it does forgiveness and reconciliation? Is it not love that replaces war with a ceasefire? Is it not love that can make two enemies become friends?

Let us be the people who carry the aura of love with us wherever we are and let us spread the aura of love to the people around us. I believe it's not by might, nor by force, nor by war, but by love that peace will prevail in our land.

Jesus says in Matthew 5:9 *"Blessed are the peacemakers."* I urge every person to come forward and work for the restoration of peace and unity wherever they're at, whether it be at a place that we live or work or socialise in. We can be people who spread love, unity and peace wherever we are, rather than people who spread hatred, destruction, violence or evil.

"Hatred stirs up dissension, but love covers over all wrongs"
(Proverbs 10:12)

Are you the carrier of peace in your society?

My Mother Suffered for Me

Dedicated to my sweet mother

Someone said "Life is short, enjoy it to the fullest." My wise mum said, "My son, the life I will have with you is all too short; I want to give you the best that I can before I am no longer in this world."

I grew up in an atmosphere where all my friends had the latest bicycle, video game or toy pistol. I always used to demand from my mother the same things my friends had, not realising that my parents were struggling to pay my school tuition fees. I still remember how my mum tried her best to give me what I desired even to the extent of borrowing money from others, just to make sure I got what I wanted.

One event is still fresh in my mind. It reminds me of how loving my mother was towards me, and how concerned she was for us, her children. It was the time that followed my dad's resignation from his job. Upon his resignation my dad started a small shop in the middle of our town to sustain my family. Life was not bad; with the shop's income - we could run our kitchen, pay for the school fees for my brother and I, and cover other expenditure. Our life was turned upside down, however, when our shop, along with other shops in the town, was burnt down by the Army after a clash between them and the Freedom Fighters. From that day forth, our family struggled with debt and a massive loss of income. It was during one of those days that my mother told me that she didn't care about herself, about buying new clothes or whether she had something good to eat. She only wished that my brother and I would not be made fun of by our friends for wearing old clothes, or be expelled from school for not being able to pay school fees. Looking back at those days, I now see how my mother worked so hard without caring what people thought about her, just to ensure I never went a day being hungry.

As I grew older and became a teenage boy, my desire for sleeping increased. Every night I would go to sleep early, leaving my mum in the kitchen trying to finish the work. In the morning I'd wake up late, only to see my mum running around tirelessly trying to finish all the household work again with no one to help her. And I, instead of giving a helping hand to my mother, would start grumbling just because the food was not up to my expectation. I can still remember the expression on my mum's face, looking at the food, discouraged, before trying to add some more ingredients to make it appetizing for me.

There was a time when I was down, discouraged and frustrated. My mum tried her best to comfort me, bearing patiently all the words I shouted at her. *Mum, I wonder how you managed to comfort me while I was trying to relieve my anger, and how you still listened to me. Mum I love you and thank God for giving me as great a mother as you.*

My mum went around borrowing money so that I would be able to study where I wanted to study. She woke up early every December morning, bearing the chilly wind, just to take care of the pig that had just given birth to piglets, so that she could get a few thousand rupees which she then sent to me as pocket money and college fees while I was studying at college.

When I come home for vacation she waited for me with her arms stretched out ready to hug me. She avoided buying new clothes for herself just in case I needed new clothes when I returned home. She sweated while working in our little kitchen garden, just to give me the best vegetables for my lunch and dinner.

What I am today is because of the tears my mother's wept for me to God. I still remember my mother praying early in the morning crying and weeping, not for herself but for me, to transform my life from bad to good.

If I were to be granted a wish from God, then I would ask God to give my mother a happy, long life, free from any more tension, because my foolishness has given her enough tension and tears to last her the rest of her life.

"And do not forsake your mother's teaching . They will be a garland to grace your head and a chain to adorn your neck"
(Proverbs 1:8b, 9)

How many times have you ever told your mum "I love you for all you have done for me?" Or are you still giving her grief?

Dear fathers or husbands, are you treating your wife well? Is she happy to tell people about you and your life together, or is she ashamed and embarrassed, being treated poorly by you?

Do you think she deserves a big hug from you, and respect for all the things she has sacrificed for you?

Dear mother! Are you playing a motherly role filled with love for your children?

Think about it!

Do You Have a Dream for a Better Tomorrow?

One of the most common questions that I remember adults asking me when I was just a small boy was, "Do you have a dream (vision or aim in life)?"

As a small boy I was not sure what they really meant when they asked me this question. I still remember answering their question in all sorts of ways. "I want to dream of Tarzan," or "My dream is to play on a beach," and so on. As I answered I would see a different reaction from each person as I answered them. Some burst into laughter, some looked at me with a weird expression on their face, and of course some well-wishers helped me to understand what they really meant by "dream".

As I grew up I remember asking my Dad one day if he still has a dream for his future, to which he replied "Martin Luther king Jr. had a dream to see black school kids and white school kids sitting together without there being any discrimination. Martin Luther King Jr.'s dream even cost him his life. But today we can see his dream came true". My dad paused for a little while and then continued to say, "Even I have a dream for the future. I have a dream that one day justice will prevail in Naga society. Common people will no longer live at the hands of a few people who hold power. There will be no more extortion, no more fear and people will be able to express their views and their rights, and fight for justice.

After many years my dad opened up and told me how he was working to fulfil those dreams. I have seen my dad receive many phone calls with threatening words; there have been attempts to kill him; people have assaulted him even in front of me. Nevertheless, I have heard my Dad say, "I may die for speaking the truth, but my work for justice will go on."

In 1774, John Adams declared his vision of a new nation, a union of 13 states. Many didn't believe that it was possible. But within two years of his declaration, the USA was born.

In 1875, England by night was lit up with gas and fire. In 1878, a person called Thomas Edison challenged his employees to come up with an electric light. Many expressed their disbelief of Thomas Edison's dream because many had tried and failed before. But after many attempts, Thomas Edison fulfilled his dream in December of 1879, when he invented the light bulb.

There are lots of people who have had dreams they have worked to fulfil. Many died for their cause and some didn't live long enough to see the results of their hard work, but in the end their dream came to pass.

No matter what people say and no matter where you come from, dare to climb the ladder of success. At the end of the day what matters most will be what you have done or achieved. Don't underestimate the potential that is within you. Keep running, keep knocking, and keep seeking until you finish the race and find what you are looking for.

"Then the Lord replied: 'write down the revelation and make it plain on tablets so that a herald may run with it. For the revelation awaits an appointed time; it speaks of the end and will not prove false. Though it linger, wait for it; it will certainly come and will not delay"
(Habakkuk 2: 2, 3)

Life is short, but the good things you do for society will be remembered and treasured by people.

Do you have a dream for a better tomorrow?

Moving Four Times in Two Years

A Lesson in Humility

Humility was one of the areas God addressed within me through different circumstances during my days in Hubli.

In June 2012, I was told by the organization with whom I was working that I was being sent to work in Hubli (Karnataka, India). I was shocked and surprised to hear this announcement as I had never before heard of Hubli. However, with much courage and determination, I accepted their proposal.

To be honest, before I went to Hubli, my imagination ran wild as I contemplated about where I would be staying. I pictured a decent house with a proper bathroom and toilet, a comfortable room where I could relax and watch television, a kitchen with a refrigerator to keep food items cool during summer and proper water facilities, and so on. But I found that everything was the opposite of what I had expected when I finally reached Hubli.

There I learned the meaning of humility and dedication. In Hubli, I learned to have a Christ-like attitude spoken of in Philippians 2:5, which says, *"Your attitude should be the same as that of Christ Jesus."* I learned to be willing to serve others and to humble myself enough to overcome obstacles and all sorts of challenges.

The Reaction from the Common People

Coping with unkind comments and encountering rude behaviour from the local people was one of the major challenges I faced. Their way of thinking and acting caused me to question my attitude. I was cheated by the shopkeepers, charged extra rupees by the auto drivers, and sometimes I was unable to decipher truth from deception. Facing these issues caused the most unbearable pain during my initial days in Hubli. At times I felt so humiliated and upset that I started questioning myself. "Am I not good enough to deserve some respect from them?" and "Who do they think I am?" were questions that plagued me.

On one occasion an auto driver was hired to take me to the train station. Before reaching the station, he suddenly stopped and asked me to give him the fare. He had not taken me where I had asked him to take me, so I was hesitant to give him the fare that we had arranged before I had even stepped into his vehicle. "Take me to the station,"

I requested. "Then I will pay you the fare we agreed upon." He refused, and instead, he asked me for the full amount.

The first thought that came to my mind was to fight with words, the second was not to give him all the money he claimed I owed, and the third was that he was cheating me because I was a non-local and new to that place. Deep inside my heart, I was hurt by his demeanour, but I chose to give him the money with a smile on my face, thank him and then walk the rest of the way to the station. As I pondered what had happened, I asked myself, "If Jesus could forgive His enemies who were killing Him, who am I to hold a grudge against that auto driver for a silly reason?"

My Four Houses in Hubli

During my two-year stay in Hubli, due to various reasons, I moved four times. At every residence, God taught me a lesson that helped me to change my attitude, my lifestyle and to trust God more, knowing that He was in control of my life.

My First House

I left Bangalore with mixed emotions. It was the place where I'd for four and a half years, and I had become very fond of it. I travelled by train to Hubli, arriving in the early hours of the morning of July 12, 2010. Accompanied by a few local people, I travelled from the train station toward my new home. My mind was occupied with the thought, "What kind of house will it be?" As we neared the area where I would be living, I looked at all of the good houses, expecting one of them to be mine. The organization for whom I worked had already arranged my accommodations in advance.

To my disappointment, we passed by all of the beautiful houses and came to a darker place. I was directed to go between the houses that led up toward a terrace. As I reached the terrace, I experienced even more mixed emotions, hoping that the small room in the corner of the terrace would not be the one designated for me. My hopes were dashed when we entered that little room, and the people accompanying me proclaimed with big smiles, "This is your room! Welcome to Hubli!" In my head, I was panicking. *"What? You mean I have to stay here in this small room, with no fan, no toilet or bathroom, barely able to breathe inside? No, I can't!"* Fortunately, I was able to swallow down this reaction and not openly express the thoughts that were swirling around in my head.

Later, as I sat alone in my room leaning against the walls of my new house, many feelings came to my mind. I started comparing my room in my parents' house with this present room. As I started to look at the provided items in the room, all I saw was dust. I looked up, longing to see a fan to turn on in the heat, but I saw none. I took a peep at the other small connected room, partitioned off by a small wall. All I saw was an old washing area that I had been told to use as a bathroom and a kitchen. For the toilet, I was instructed to go downstairs where I would have to share with a family. Needless to say, this particular lack of convenience was very difficult for me to digest. The worst bit of news was the owner informing me not to use water lavishly as there was a lack of water there. I still remember how often I had to fill buckets and run around, taking the water here and there.

Still, as the days went by, I started to enjoy living in that little room, with the kids around. By the time I was told that I would have to move, I was so settled that the thought of changing residences greatly saddened me. I had learned so many lessons in my short time there. The greatest lesson I had learned was to keep my belongings organised and clean in a small and crowded environment. I had grown so attached and fond of that little place, that I found it was hard for me to move away.

Second House

The colony I was living in was in a good location; I lived near the railway station, bus stand and the bazaar. However, it meant that it was very difficult to find a house for rent in that area and the organisation I was working with struggled to find a better room for me.

On August 20th 2010, I shifted from my little room to my next house. The new house was spacious, with two bedrooms, a common room, kitchen and bathroom, and even a toilet attached. It was a big old house made of wood and bricks, meaning it needed a good spring clean upon arrival. The master bedroom was in particular need of a clean. Thankfully my cousin was with me that day, so we set off to work the whole day. Late at night we finally took a step back and admired all our hard work. Satisfied with the development we saw, we made our beds and promptly fell asleep.

I was sleeping very deeply until suddenly in my dream I saw myself trying to swim in a big river. My hand became stuck in my shirt and I was struggling to free myself until I was woken by my cousin's voice, telling me that it was raining heavily and our house was full of water. He wasn't wrong; to my surprise, as I got up I found that my clothes were dripping wet and almost the whole house was flooded. It was at that moment, standing in a big puddle of water in my room that I realised how blessed people are who have shelter to protect them from the weather. It was through this incident I learnt to thank God for the shelter He had provided me. For me, there was water leakage just because there were some holes in the roof of the house, but for some they don't have that comfort. There are people who struggle day and night in the scorching sun, heavy rain and cold nights without any shelter. Who am I that the Lord of all the earth has blessed me with shelter and all daily needs? This was a turning point in my life that changed my perspective towards the beggars I saw on the streets.

Learnt to work hard

Things like cleaning, washing clothes and cooking were some of the last options I would have opted for, had I been given the chance to choose how I lived, but in Hubli those things came as compulsory duties for me. They were unavoidable; "Do or die" were the options. I remember the days that I'd wish God would send an Angel to do those things for me. However, as I look back at those days I realise they've become fond and, fun-filled memories of mine that I doubt I'll forget throughout my lifetime.

I was holding the designations of every person in a family. Like a father whose duty was to make sure that needs were met for the family; like a mother whose duty was to make sure that the house was clean, the food was cooked, the children were clean and happy and their clothes were washed. I was also like a small kid in the family who had to eat whatever was laid on the table, who dirtied his clothes constantly, only to add to the pile that needed washing, and who demanded special food from time to time, just to feel a little more satisfied with what he had.

Cleaning the house

My first house was quite a small one, so when it came to cleaning it didn't take me long, but the new house I shifted to was very big, and quickly looked like a storehouse if I didn't clean for more than a couple of days. The big tree that stood behind the house contributed a lot towards bringing dust into my house. Sometimes I'd curse the tree for all the inconvenience it caused me and often missed my old house when it came to keeping things clean.

Nevertheless, I always had company when I cleaned the big old house. The smart cockroaches, the spiders that made lovely cobwebs, the ants that seemed to get everywhere, the mosquitoes that clearly thought I was very sweet and the rats that scuttled around my bed each night. They always tested my patience while cleaning the house. They were like small children who made a mess wherever they went, and I was like a mother who had to clean up after them. I still remember being up in the middle of the night sometimes, playing chase with rats that would find their way under my blanket or run endlessly around my mattress that lay on the floor as there was no bed for me to sleep on. The room would be sounded by THUMPs and TICK, TACK, BANG noises as I'd try and hit them with whatever hard object lay closest to me at the time.

Oh, how I miss those sweet old days.

Washing clothes

"If you want to wear clean clothes then you better wash them clean."

Washing was another of the big challenges I faced while living alone. " I hardly get time to cook, clean, do my personal studying, go out to the field and go to different meetings, so when will I find time to wash my clothes?" This was a question I always asked myself when I saw the clothes piling up, waiting for me to wash by hand. Sometimes I'd get fed up and give up half way through my pile, but I knew the washing didn't wash itself and I'd have to come back to it again later.

By the end of my stay in Hubli, I'd adopted different methods of hand washing my clothes, and didn't mind so much that there wasn't a machine as I'd learnt to wash quickly and well.

Cooking food

Unlike most places where people said "how are you?" as one of the common questions, I found that the most common question people asked me in Hubli was "How do you cook yourself?" to which I'd humorously reply "I don't cook myself but I cook rice, noodles, meat and vegetables". In fact, although I enjoyed cooking, it became one of the most difficult tasks I faced. If I didn't cook, then I'd have to either starve or eat at a restaurant. The latter option was usually ruled out, as my low salary usually didn't make it feasible and coming from a different culture meant I couldn't find the foods I was used to at restaurants.

On many occasions I'd come home late at night after a long day, and before I could relax, I'd have to put the rice on to cook. Thankfully, I was blessed to have to an electric rice cooker, which meant all I had to do was get the measurements correct and let the cooker do the rest. However, I'd then have to ask myself another question: "What curry shall I prepare tonight?" Different options would run through my head as I tried to decide: "Quick-boiled vegetables? It is quick, but that doesn't sound very tasty. Ok, how about chicken? Yes, that sounds yummy. But then I'll have to chop onions, potatoes, tomatoes and chillies and I'm too tired to go to all that effort and moreover I forgot to stock up on my Masala the last time I went to the bazaar."

People who knew me often made comments about my living, saying they'd never seen someone like me who would only cook to fill the stomach, not caring so much about how the food tasted. God was so gracious that on many of those late nights when I thought I'd have to come home to cook, He'd send food to me through someone else, providing for me just when I needed His provision. God's grace was always with me and His strength was what kept me going through all the challenges that I faced, and later they even became a source of joy.

Saved from a fallen tree

As I mentioned earlier, there were many holes in the roof of the big old house that I stayed in and it led to puddles of water being formed inside the house every time it rained. The house owner tried to repair the roof many times but somehow the water still kept leaking in and I'd have to run around searching for the bucket to keep in the spot that was leaking every time the heavens opened. Sometimes it leaked so much that no matter how many buckets I had it would never be enough, and I'd have to stay awake all night, standing in one corner of the room, just to protect myself as everything else got soaked. After many months of battling this problem I decided to move my bedroom downstairs to the common room.

There were times I'd complain to God for taking me through those events and I found it hard to understand why such things were happening to me. One night as I was sleeping in the common room downstairs I heard a big "BANG". I woke up startled as the sound seemed so close, after looking around and lying awake for a few minutes to see if anything else happened, I dozed off again. After a while, I was woken again, this time by the sound of people outside my house, I got out of bed and stumbled, half dazed, towards the door. I was fully awake as soon as people gasped to see me standing at the doorway. Questions started flying in my direction "Are you ok?", and "Are you hurt?" Confused, I asked them what was going on, and their response was just to look up and point at the roof of my house. I followed their fingers, landing my eyes on what used to be the roof of my house, destroyed by the big tree that had once stood tall behind it and was now lying sideways over my house. In shock, I climbed the steps to the first floor and stood gazing around me at the tiles and branches all over what had recently been my bedroom. The only thing I could think at that moment was "God, thank you for saving me." I realised then that if the roof hadn't leaked for all those months, then I would have still been sleeping there, and would currently be crushed by the tree, and the roof, as I lay asleep in my bed.

At that moment I changed my attitude. I asked forgiveness from God for all the times I'd complained to Him about the water leaking into my room, and instead thanked God for letting the water leak in my room as I knew he'd actually been protecting me from the greater problem that was to come– being crushed to death by a tree. All I could say in the days and months that followed that incident was "Great is Thy faithfulness."

"The Lord keeps you from all harm and watches over your life" (Psalm 121:7)

Third House

After my second house was severely damaged, I spent a couple of weeks or more sleeping at one of my neighbour's houses. That was until a man approached me one day and asked me if I could stay in his furnished house as he and his family were moving to another city. With much joy and excitement I accepted his request and moved over to their house. It was wonderful! It had all the proper facilities and furniture I'd been imagining before I'd ever moved to Hubli.

It was then that I looked back on all the experiences I'd had since moving to Hubli and thanked God for all His blessings that He'd been showering upon me, and for the fact that He was moulding me and shaping me to be a better person. All those experiences had taught me to trust in Him daily and through every circumstance.

Time was flying by, I was continually seeing God's hand upon my life and continued to thank Him for all that He'd given me and for the shelter He'd provided me with. However, one fine morning about seven months after I'd moved into the wonderful house, the house owner called me and told me he was sorry to say that I had to move out because his family was returning to Hubli and needed their home back. Though it was overwhelming to hear this news at first, I took it in a positive way knowing that good things were still to come.

I was so blessed to have a lot of local friends from that area, and they helped me search for a new place to live. They managed to find a small room on the terrace of one of the family homes not far from where I'd been staying. So, once again, with the help of my friends, I moved to a new house. When I saw the room, I immediately had flashbacks about the first house, but this time instead of panicking I smiled and told myself "this is beautiful."

I quickly thanked the friends who helped me move and the family who had welcomed me so warmly and provided the room free of charge. Again, God was blessing me and providing me with not only shelter, but with wonderful, supportive people.

Fourth house

It was mid-summer when I moved into my fourth house, with a temperature averaging 37-42 degrees Celsius. Staying on a terrace in a small, tin-roofed room, with only a table fan to keep me cool, was not my idea of fun. But, I'd learnt from my previous experiences and refused to allow myself to be discouraged. Instead, I'd make a point to thank God for a room with a roof that protected me from the scorching heat of the sun and from the monsoon rain.

A few days after I'd moved in, the lady who came to wash clothes for the owner of my house came and offered to wash my clothes and dirty vessels too. Not even a week later another lady approached me to tell me she'd watched me going out to work, coming home late and then cooking for myself. She said she felt sorry for me and wanted to help, so she started cooking extra and sending me breakfast, lunch and even dinner almost every day.

I look back at the time I spent in my second house, where I'd spent all my free time cleaning the house, washing clothes, cooking and washing the vessels. And then I look at the time I spent in my fourth house, where I cooked and cleaned often, not because I had to any more, but because I'd learnt to love to. My attitude and behaviour had turned 180 degrees between those two houses. Looking back at those two years of my life I realise how much God was teaching me and preparing me in so many ways to be more capable in every area of my life and to trust Him more and more.

"Those who trust in the Lord will find new strength"
(Isaiah 40: 31)

Moving myself and all my belongings four times in those two years in Hubli was not easy. Many times, I questioned God and questioned myself, but I began to realise that everything happens for a reason. God often puts us into challenging situations, not to belittle us but to help us to learn and make us stronger. I went to Hubli for one year but I ended up staying two years. I will always cherish the experiences that taught me to know, love, and trust God more and more in every circumstance.

As I have mentioned at the beginning of this chapter, during my initial days in Hubli I was very negative about the place and the people. By the time I left Hubli, I'd learnt that not everyone was the same; not every auto driver or shopkeeper cheated me; not every person was rude to me and not a single one of my homes turned out to be a complete disaster. In fact, I became friends with some of the greatest people I'd ever met, and I'd come to love each of my homes and each of my experiences.

So are you finding it hard to understand why something is happening in your life? Do you feel hopeless like you're stuck in a rut and you can't get out of a situation? Draw closer to God, trust Him, share your worries and struggles with Him and wait patiently for Him to reveal His plan and purpose for you. I guarantee He will.

"He has made everything beautiful in its time"
(Ecclesiastes 3:11)

Lessons Learnt from a Tree

One day I was thinking about how amazing it is that a small seed can turn into a huge tree. As I was pondering this mystery, a lot of other thoughts came to mind. One was how different kinds of seeds sprout different creations. Some trees produce fruits of which there are many different shapes, sizes, tastes and colours, while others don't produce any fruit but still look magnificent. I also noticed that some fruit-bearing trees bear fruit or segments without seeds, while some fruits have small seeds, and others have one giant seed in the middle. If we observe the cycle of a tree, it's wonderful to see how a small seed goes through so many changes before the fruit is produced.

For a seed to grow, it first has to battle against the soil in order to make its way out of the ground. In the initial years, dealing with the weather is one of the tree's hardest battles; it has to endure wind and rain that, when forceful, could knock it down or break its branches.

Insects can be another test for a tree to overcome. But if the shrub is strong enough it can withstand the challenges it faces and become a beautiful, blossoming tree. Once it's grown its leaves, and its flowers have bloomed, the tree is able to produce fruit.

I believe that, even as humans, we go through a cycle in order to become the person we're aiming to be. Just like a tree, we battle against different obstacles throughout our lives. Children have to learn how to walk, stumbling and injuring themselves time and time again before they finally achieve their goal. As they grow, they have to face different fears and challenges, like going to school for the first time, making friends and learning new lessons both in and outside of school. Then, again, as they grow a little older they may even battle against laziness, feelings of inferiority, fear and rejection, and experience the loss of loved ones, depression, anxiety and financial worries. All these challenges can affect our lives, our self-esteem and our belief in ourselves, and can deter us from having a goal and working hard to achieve it.

Just as a tree stands against the storms, so must we be prepared to stand up against every obstacle, challenge or discouragement that may cross our path as we walk through life. Like a tree, we can stand strong with a firm foundation to overcome the hurdles.

Know where you're going, know why you're going, and then, you'll have more than 1,001 reasons to say why you're not giving up on what you're doing.

I Played a Lullaby
for my Friend

Who would have ever imagined that a few humorous words would fall on the ground as a seed and grow tall enough to come to pass?

I still remember a day in my college, in Bangalore, India, back in 2007, when I was trying to find my hostel room. One fine afternoon, at the beginning of a new semester, everyone was busy looking at the notice- board, trying to find their new hostel room number as the institution moved all the students around every year. I squeezed my way through the crowd until I could catch a glimpse of my name and room number on the list: "Limaonen, Room no.53." Immediately, I turned and squeezed my way back out of the mass of students, to head towards my new room. As I exited the crowd I saw a tall, fair, huge guy walking at a fast pace towards me. My first thought was to jump out of the way to make sure the guy didn't fall over me, but thankfully he slowed to a halt as he neared. He asked my name and when I told him, he followed on by introducing himself as my new roommate. As we headed off to find room no.53 together he told me that a friend of mine who was already studying there had directed him to me.

Our room was much like all the others and my new roommate seemed pleasant. After a few days, I took my sweet old harmonica out to play a lullaby. As I was playing I saw my roommate watching me in amazement. As the song came to an end, he told me that he'd been longing to learn how to play the harmonica for a long time. And so, from that night forth, our classes began. Very soon after, he bought a new harmonica for himself and put in a lot of effort to play the best lullaby he possibly could. Unfortunately his practise didn't please himself or the other hostellers within hearing range. An agreement was quickly made that if he stopped playing, I would play a lullaby at his wedding.

A year went by, and the time came for my roommate to leave the college. Three years later I was leaving college too, ready to embark on a new adventure to a city about 470km from Bangalore. I went to Hubli, Karnataka, to stay there for a couple of years and work with an organisation. Little did I know that I'd be bumping into that old roommate, and that Hubli was his home town. We reminisced over days gone by and our time studying in Bangalore. About two months later I received a call from my friend with some great news: he was getting married. He reminded me of the promise I'd made four years before, and without taking a breath I accepted his request to play a lullaby music piece for him on his special day.

It was a great wedding day; everyone was excited, happy, smiling and laughing as they celebrated together. I walked onto the stage, remembering all those days that my roommate and I had spent together, and couldn't believe how our humorous deal had turned into reality. As I was about to play, I looked at my roommate with his beautiful bride by his side. It reminded me of our bachelor days, and I said to myself "Oh, man, you're not a bachelor anymore" as I began to play. I played the best I could and with a smile on my face I looked at him again as the piece came to an end and I exited the stage.

Now he's a dad, but whenever we meet he still behaves just as he was when we were roommates.

Treasure your friends no matter how far the distance and how regularly you can meet. As life goes by, we make new friends as we go from school to college, college to university, university to a job, or from place to place. But one thing that is always worth doing is keeping in touch with old friends or new and helping one another in times of need. For me, having a circle of friends around me is one of the most beautiful treasures that I can keep in life apart from my family.

I encourage you to take five minutes out of your day to make a call to a friend you've not been in touch with for a while but have many great memories of and see their reaction. Who knows, it might be the renewal of your bond of friendship again.

*"A man of many companions may come to ruin, but there is a
friend who sticks closer than a brother"*
(Proverbs 18: 24)

**True friends remain the same though everything around
them may change.**

Drowning my Attitude

Who would ever have thought that being a bachelor staying far away from home and living in a different culture would be a good life? I thought it would be, but in reality, it was tough. I had to adjust to different foods; encounter different tastes when it came to cooking; and get used to washing clothes, cleaning the house and making sure that everything was in order. I was always busy running here and there only to come home late at night after work and find that the vessels don't cook food for themselves and that I didn't have enough money to eat in a restaurant every night. I'd go window shopping, where my mind would always have to concentrate on kitchen stuff, like whether I needed more rice, tomatoes, potatoes and onions and so on, rather than on new clothes or perfume – that would usually be the first priority for people my age.

I still remember going window shopping with friends at Big Bazaar. The first things they would set eyes on would be the rails of clothes. They'd browse through and then ask me which one was better out of the few that they liked. Instead of answering their question my mind would be on what I needed to buy for the house and I'd go on to tell them the list of groceries I needed to get. Many times my friends looked at me with a confused expression and would say to each other: "Leave him alone, he's partially married with no wife."

Hanging out at night was the best part of my time in Hubli. I had some of the most unforgettable moments during those times with friends from Hubli, riding with them on their bikes. But no matter how much fun I was having, at the back of my mind that I'd always be thinking that I'd have to cook again when I got home. I remember telling my friend, "Oh, I need to cook once I get back home" when they told me they needed to get back and have their dinner.

There were many occasions like that, when I'd realise my life was tougher than the lives of others. There was once a time my friend exclaimed, "Oh, I forgot to give my clothes for laundry" and I responded by saying, "Oh, I forgot to wash my clothes" (that I'd have to do by hand, not with a washing machine). Whenever they'd say "Hush, I forgot to tell my servant to clean my room," I'd exclaim "Hush, I forgot to clean my room."

I thought life was always a struggle when I was away from home, doing everything that I'd never expected to do, but one day a friend of mine knocked on my head– knock, knock, and knock! And it was at that moment I realised how negatively I was thinking. I realised that everything I thought negatively about made me sad or frustrated or angry and that I didn't have to think and feel that way. So I taught myself to start thinking positively. As I started looking at all the things I was doing at that time and in that place, I told myself: "Life is all around me." I began to feel confident when I thought of the future ahead of me; because I could see what I was learning then would help me to be a more responsible person in the future.

From that day forth, I started changing my attitude and looking at the things around me in a different way, and as I did this I started enjoying everything I did, whether it was in my job or at home. I often used to tell myself: "Lima, one day you will miss these moments so enjoy everything you are doing here." And yes, indeed, by the time I came to writing this story I did miss those beautiful moments I spent working and running here and there, and the moments I spent in my small room all alone with all the provisions God had given me through unexpected ways.

I've come to realise that it is our attitude that decides whether you look back at your past with a smile on your face or with regret in your heart, and also whether you look forward to the future with optimism or with fear.

"Surely your goodness and unfailing love will pursue me all the days of my life" (Psalm 23:6)

Things around us will change. They will become better and more meaningful if our attitude towards things around us changes in a positive way.

Things around us will change. They will become better and more meaningful if our attitude towards things around us changes in a positive way.

My Journey towards Germany

"G"ermany?"

"Yes, Germany!"

My friend paused for a second, a concerned expression forming on his face "But you've only got a few weeks until the course starts– isn't it too late to apply for a visa? I heard that to obtain a German Visa it takes at least around 8 to 10 weeks to process it as they send all the documents to Germany, and you don't even have all the necessary documents with you here in Hubli."

The moment I heard that I had been selected to pursue a six-month course in Germany, I started to prepare all the documents required to obtain my visa. It would be my first time travelling abroad, and I had very little knowledge about the procedure. The first thing I did was call my parents because all my documents were in my hometown, which was over 4,000 kilometres away from Hubli. I still remember how frustrating it was trying to get all the correct documents. I received my one-month bank statement a week after calling my parents, only to discover that one month was too short. I, therefore, had to ask my parents to go to the bank for a second time. They got a signed and sealed three-month statement and sent it to me. Another week went by, and I received my new one, only to find that this, too, was incorrect, as I needed a six-month statement. I requested that my parents go to the bank for a third time, and I waited in anticipation for a week as the statement was sent down to me. Thankfully, this time, there were no problems.

After a great deal of hassle, including running around to obtain the necessary paperwork and meeting several times with the agent who was trying to help me, I managed to make an appointment for the submission of my application and my visa interview.

Finally, the day came for my interview, which would be held in Bangalore, India. As I entered the room to submit my application to the German consulate, I thought to myself, *well, at last the day has come that will decide my fate.* But my excitement and confidence faded quickly as I realised that I had not sorted two very important documents—my medical insurance and the tickets for my flight. All I had was my passport, an invitation letter from the school in Germany and a few other documents. With a heavy heart, I told myself, *I can't do anything at the moment, so may His (God's) will be done.* When it was my turn to be interviewed, I entered the office without much hope. This is when the consulate informed me that my agent had made an appointment for the wrong person and that my interview was cancelled. For a moment, I felt as if a big stone had hit me in the head, and thereafter, frustration plagued my every thought.

I contacted my agent, who managed to make the correct appointment for the following day. The next day, I attended the interview again, knowing that my luck was bad and that I did not have the complete set of documents and that would decrease my chances of being granted a visa. I entered the building and patiently awaited my turn to re-submit my documents. I could hear the questions they were asking the person ahead of me—about insurance, whether he knew the German language and so on—and, again, my confidence dropped. Deep inside my heart, I said to myself, *Oh, Lima, you are doomed.* However, when it was my turn and the consulate called my name, she knew that she had mispronounced it, and she started to laugh. Her mood changed in an instant, and she started a conversation with me, asking me how to say my name correctly and which part of India I was from. She then took my documents and asked me only two questions: "Do you need the original documents back?" and "Can you tell me something about the school you're going to?" After hearing my brief answers, she looked at me with a smile and said, "All the best for your studies. We'll notify you when your passport is ready." A massive smile formed on my face, and deep within my heart, I felt like jumping with joy. I told myself, *Lima, you are the luckiest man on Earth*!

Six weeks later, by which time I was back in my hometown, I was still waiting for my passport. With only ten days until school started, I told my father that my visa was unlikely to arrive in time and that I felt that I should cancel my flight. I had booked a ticket from Nagaland to Bangalore but still had not booked my flight from Bangalore to Germany, as I was not 100% certain that my plans would all work out. That night, I logged in to my email to send a message to the school to explain what was happening with my visa. However, to my surprise, I saw an email from the school leader in Germany informing me that he had gone to the embassy in Germany to find out what was happening and that they had informed him that my visa had been granted and were waiting for me to collect it in Bangalore. I screamed with joy and ran to tell my parents the news. I immediately started looking at flights tickets. I was hoping to book a ticket to Munich, the city nearest the school, but after discovering it was double the cost of a flight to Frankfurt, which was a bit further away, I decided to go with the cheaper option.

Finally, it was time for me to fly to Germany. I was told that after I reached Germany, I would need to take a train from Frankfurt Airport to the nearest train station from my destination (Hurlach). Because this was my first trip abroad, I worried about everything, not realising that God knows how to do it all. I was fearful when someone told me that the immigration officer might ask to see my return ticket and my medical insurance. The other worry I had was about the trains: how would I purchase a train ticket, how would I know that I was boarding the correct train and how would I know when I would have to change trains?

Having reached Bangalore and collected my passport, I started the first leg of my journey, flying from Bangalore to Delhi. I reached Delhi Airport, and with a few hours to wait until my next flight, I decided to wander around inside. While exploring, I met a gentleman who happened to be waiting for the same flight that I was on, so we decided to travel together. He assured me that he would help me purchase a train ticket once we reached Frankfurt, which was very comforting to hear.

Upon arrival in Frankfurt, I started to tremble as I waited in line to face the immigration officer. When it was my turn, the officer took a quick glance at me and asked to see my passport and invitation letter. The fear faded as he stamped my passport and called to the next person in line to step forward. I was so relieved that the most challenging part of my journey was over and that everything had gone smoothly. The gentleman whom I met in Delhi helped me book a train ticket, which was another great relief, as everything was written in German, and I do not think I would have been able to figure it out by myself. He then called the staff of my school and gave them the details of my train: the train number and the time it would be arriving at my destination.

Worry crept back in again as he explained to me that I would have to change trains at three different stations. As it was my first time on a foreign train in a foreign land where a foreign language was spoken, and I didn't know how the system worked there, I started to panic. My friend tried to explain everything, and he assured me that it would be fine. I thanked him, and we said goodbye.

I still remember how I ran from one platform to another, not really knowing what I was doing, looking at the train times and numbers and then just jumping on, often with less than a minute to spare before the train left the platform. Thankfully, I managed to get on the right trains on time, and I reached my final destination (unlike one incident that occurred later during my time in Germany, when a group of us boarded the wrong train). I was met by a lady who was waiting for me at the station, and I breathed a sigh of relief. I had made it! As I started to recount the journey, I realised how amazing it was that everything had gone smoothly and how God had miraculously helped me throughout the process, from my application right up until the moment I had arrived. A smile graced my lips; I knew it was only the beginning.

When I look back at all those times of frustration and discouragement and at the times when I felt like just giving up on my preparation for my trip to Germany, all I can say is "*Great is Thy faithfulness!*"

"Commit to God whatever you do and your plans will succeed" (Proverbs 16:3)

Are you worried about something today? Do you feel something's impossible and you want to give up? I would say "give your worries, problems, plans and everything to God and let Him do wonders in your life."

"Cast all your anxiety on him because he cares for you"
(1 Peter 5:7)

An Encounter with a Boy from the Amazon Rainforest

It was December of the year 2012 when a few of my friends and I embarked on our journey from Germany to Brazil. We had a few places in mind to visit while in Brazil. The first being Manaus, north of the country. During our time in Manaus we often visited different villages inside the Amazon Rainforest to interact with the people, and help them in any way we could. Sometimes we worked together with them on their farm. Sometimes we'd bring wood from deep within the forest to the village to build their house. Other times we'd help clean their surroundings and so forth. Life in the Amazon Rainforest was indeed full of surprises. We never knew what we'd be seeing or doing next. I experienced a mix of different emotions during my time there. Fear crept in from time to time, but there was also something exciting about being in a forest of which I'd heard so much about. Mosquitoes were the least of our problems. Bites from ants and other insects would give some sort of allergic reaction and the heat and humidity was almost unbearable. But whatever the hardships, we took everything as an experience and took every challenge positively. We continually reminded ourselves that our trip was a once in a lifetime opportunity and something so worthwhile.

Visiting and interacting with different villages and tribes were some of the best moments I had in the Amazon. During my visit I also noticed that there were many similarities between the tribal people of Amazon and my own people (the Nagas). I especially noticed the similarities between what we use in our home or on our farms. I was often mistaken for being one of them because of my appearance. Another common thing I observed and heard from most of the people in the forest was that they were happy to be there, rather than living in a developed city. I saw how people loved one another, cared for one another, shared things with one another and had a heart of hospitality.

One day my friends and I visited another village inside the forest. As we reached the village the children came running to us and around us, trying to talk to us. As most of us couldn't speak their language it was difficult for us to speak to them. During our conversations with the people we were always helped by our guides, who translated for us. As I was trying to talk to the children in that particular village, I was captivated by the sweet smile of a boy who looked up at me when we met. He looked so happy and cheerful. I asked our translator to tell me more about the 6 year old boy.

As our translator told us about the boy's background and who he was, I listened intently. The boy happened to have a speech impairment (meaning he couldn't speak properly), but still he was so much more joyful than the other children in the same village. I asked my translator about how the boy felt about his physical challenge. He replied that the boy always smiled and was cheerful even though he could not speak to anyone. Watching the little boy with the beaming smile led me to change my entire perspective in just those few minutes. I learnt from that little boy that I should be joyful always and not let my weaknesses undermine me. I needed to appreciate what I had and carry a smile, thinking positively about my life.

Encountering this small boy has taught me a great lesson which I hadn't learnt anywhere else. Meeting him and knowing the truth about him has revolutionized my whole idea of who I am in God's eyes. I know no matter how I look, walk, talk, etc. in God's eyes I am beautiful.

I don't know if I will ever be able to meet this small boy again in this journey of life, but the impact he made on me will not leave me until my last breath.

As you read about this boy may you realise how beautiful you are in God's eyes and enjoy every moment with thanksgiving to God. Don't let your weaknesses (physical problems, sickness, talents, and so on) put you down. Just because people say you can't doesn't mean you can't. There is a God that says "you can."

*"I praise you because I am fearfully and wonderfully made;
your works are wonderful, I know that full well"*
(Psalm 139:14)

**Don't let anyone make you feel unworthy or inferior by
the way you approach them.**

Journey Well

Life comes as a package. As our life unravels itself it's full of all sorts of surprises: joy, sorrow, hurt, love, fear, disappointment, failure, loneliness, achievements and many more. For every individual, girl or a boy, rich or poor, young or old, strong or weak, graduate or non-graduate before we take our last breathe on this journey, we will surely experience all of these emotions.

As I grew up I remember observing the lifestyles of anyone who was older than me, be they my teachers, parents, youth leaders or someone else. I used to admire some of them for the good qualities they possessed and wanted to be like them, but for some reason I used to tell my friends that I would never actually be like them as their lifestyles were not so acceptable to society. So just like I used to notice the lifestyle of people around me, I realise now that the same thing may be happening to me – others may be directly or indirectly observing my life. I need to be wise in how I behave, because, at the end of the day, my character or lifestyle will define who I am in society. I want people to remember me as having lived life truthfully, honestly, and free from corruption, having maintained my integrity.

I want people to remember me for my punctuality, my generosity, my humility and my kind heart.

Our life is like a story book; I want people to see and remember my story, to learn from the good, positive things I did, and I'm sure you would want the same for your life. I doubt many people would want to finish their story in a negative way and be remembered for immorality, hatred, selfishness, pride and so on. I believe no matter how powerful a person is, how much they possess and how intelligent they are, at the end of the journey no one will escape "Death". It's up to us to write a story with our lives that will teach the next generation greater and more positive things than our own generation has known.

I believe when someone dies people react in different ways depending on who they were. Upon a person's death, people come together and share stories and memories of the one they've just lost. Many people are full of love, gratitude and awe as they look back on their loved one's life, and there is often a sadness that comes with losing that special person. But for others, it's easy to think negatively of the person who has died and continue to speak and think badly about them, basing their thoughts and feelings on what that person was like during their life journey.

One day I happened to attend two different funerals. As I reached the first place I heard people say a lot of negative things about the person who had died. What was even more depressing was that even during the relatives' funeral speeches they told the people attending not to be like the deceased; otherwise they'd face the same consequences. Following that funeral I went to attend the second one; the atmosphere here was very different. People were talking about how unfortunate it was for the family and the society as a whole that the person had died. They shared different reminiscent memories of the deceased and were full of sorrow at the loss.

I wonder, if you or I died today, how would people react?

Let us try to live life in such a way that when we die people will miss us for all the good things we have done, both for individuals and for the welfare of society. And most importantly, if we're breathing our last breaths, will we be able to say as Paul said: *"I have fought the good fight, I have finished the race" (2 Timothy 4:7)*

One day someone might read your life. So journey well that your life journal will be worth reading and will inspire others to have hope and confidence in themselves.

"What good will it be for a man if he gains the whole world, yet forfeits his soul" (Matthew 16:26a)

Life is short but our story will go on.